# Free From Captivity

A Memoir of a Generational Curse Breaker

By

Shawnee Palmer, LCSW, LAC

Free From Captivity
Copyright © 2023 by Shawnee Palmer

First Printing, 2023
ISBN: 978-1-7355688-2-9

Alpine's Empowerment Agency
7014 Smith Corners Blvd, #1198
Charlotte, NC 28269
www.alpinesempowermentagency.com

Unless specifically stated, all scripture references taken from the Holy Bible, New International Version®, NIV® Copyright ©1973, 1978, 1984, 2011 by Biblica, Inc.® Used by permission. All rights reserved worldwide.

***All rights reserved.*** No part of this publication may be reproduced, stored in a retrieval system, or transmitted, in any form or by any means, electronic, digital, mechanical, photocopying, recording or otherwise, without the prior written permission of the publisher.

*Dedication*
*To Jesus, thank you for saving my life!*

# Table of Contents

| | |
|---|---|
| **Prelude** | vii |
| **Chapter One** | 1 |
| **Chapter Two** <br> Pieces of My Backstory | 7 |
| **Chapter Three** <br> God is the Truth, Be True to You | 15 |
| **Chapter Four** <br> God's Grace is Sufficient | 23 |
| **Chapter Five** <br> God is a Healer | 31 |
| **Chapter Six** <br> He Brings Peace | 39 |
| **Chapter Seven** <br> He is a Great Provider & Deliverer | 47 |
| **Chapter Eight** <br> Get to Know Jesus; He is Victorious! | 57 |

**Chapter Nine**      **65**
    Deliverance Is Free for All; He is Mighty!

**Chapter Ten**      **71**
    When You're Tired & Have Tried EVERYTHING, Try Jesus!

**Chapter Eleven**      **79**
    The Power of Repentance

**Chapter Twelve**      **87**
    Don't Delay Your Deliverance

**Chapter Thirteen**      **95**
    Friendships Change After Deliverance

**Chapter Fourteen**      **101**
    What Are You Willing to Sacrifice for Your FREEDOM?

# Prelude

As I was acquainting myself with the Holy Spirit, he began to impart to me what setting the captives free meant. I had been consistently hearing the word and seeing YouTube videos with the title in them, that I had to inquire about the relevancy of it in my life. I needed to know what I was supposed to do with this information and, most importantly, how to partner with God to fulfill it. As a mental health therapist, I understand the aspects of what it's like for one to experience PTSD, but I didn't understand what that looked like on a spiritual level. Then the Holy Spirit began to minister to me about the different levels of consciousness one goes through when they are detached from their bodies and in a state of fear while reliving a horrific memory from the past. In the mental health field, it's called dissociation. Many individuals experience this if something in their present environment triggers a memory which can happen through any use of the five senses. For example, if a person was in a severe car accident where a blue car hit them, the color blue could be a trigger that catapults them back into the time period where that accident happened within a matter of seconds. I am learning that in the spiritual realm, the visual of what takes place with a trigger is dependent on how we respond to it. For instance, if a person decides to entertain the trigger with fear, it can cause one to be trapped, reliving the experience for a matter of seconds, minutes, days, or weeks. It honestly just depends on that person's level of sensitivity to the event. Typically, when they are re-experiencing it, they have an intense emotion that latches onto them that holds them hostage until they find a way to free themselves from it. In the mental health field, we will call it "learning how to manage our emotions." This is often a task that we must learn as humans since we were all born to have feelings. If one isn't taught how to properly manage their emotions from a young age, then it can be challenging for them to manage them as an adult. In my opinion, adulthood is the beginning of the application of all the tools we learned about life during our childhood. Many individuals did not have access to healthy role models, so the people that played a role in their lives naturally passed down what they did have, which may have come from a poverty mindset. Overall, once you're an adult, you are 100% responsible for your life, and guess what? People will hold you to each responsibility despite what tools you are starting with. Setting the captives free is a guide for you to identify where you've been held captive, on what offenses you have been held bound to, and how to partner with God to release yourself from it. The only way that I know how to guide anyone is through sharing my own testimony. I pray that this book inspires you to set yourself free, become all that God has called you to be, and partner with God to help set others free. My favorite saying is, "Each one, teach one," so let's get to work!

# Chapter One

*Jeremiah 33:7 (NIV) I will bring Judah and Israel back from captivity and will rebuild them as they were before.*

Not too long ago, I was held bound and accused of offenses that were beyond my comprehension. It's one thing to be aware of the poor choices you have made, but it's another to be completely blinded by them in a way you have normalized them. When I think of an offense, I look at the list of things that you can be accused of in court, such as theft, money laundering, kidnapping, assault, reckless driving, stalking, shoplifting, and the list goes on and on. I have always been conscious of the decisions that I made to avoid getting into trouble with the law. In school and in my community growing up, these things were evident as police officers would come to our schools to share with us about the law and the dangers of breaking the law. I mean, I was well aware of what not to do and made it a daily mission to not. While I am not perfect, I always worked on being perfect, but we know that everyone can fall short. There were many occasions where I made poor choices, and they came with big consequences, but I took ownership of them and felt at peace once time passed by.

The problem with being held bound and accused of offenses that I was experiencing was that they were accusations made by Satan, the enemy, towards me and not just me but my whole bloodline and the ancestors that came before me. When I learned about these offenses I also learned about how covenants and curses work. Then I had an instant revelation about the laws of the spiritual realm that no one, and I mean no one talked about during my upbringing. I would hear certain phrases such as "what goes around, comes around" as a child, and I eventually understood it because I would see people do good and good come back around and the same with bad. But some people were doing bad, and good kept coming their way. I honestly viewed myself as being a good person that had bad things come my way. I just couldn't quite put my finger on why this was happening to me. I soon learned the meaning of being held captive for offenses committed by my ancestors and, of course, me.

The short version of being held captive is exactly what it sounds like, one who is thrown in prison for a crime they've committed. The only difference here is that the spiritual version of this ranges from a plethora of scenarios. I will discuss some scenarios in this book because I've personally experienced them; for others, I will have to refer you to the Bible. Either way it goes, being in captivity is no fun when you think you're innocent. I mean, why would you be guilty of something that you weren't aware was even an offense? Well, this is how many of us slip up in the world by doing what everyone else is doing and thinking the way everyone else is thinking. I wish I could say that the offenses are that clear and simple, but they are much more complex than that.

As complex as it may sound, no one is exempt from being held captive. There are many scenarios of mothers, fathers, and children suffering because of generational curses. I was a child that suffered and was held captive by the decisions of my forefathers. How do I know that? Well, when I started to read the Bible while fasting and praying, God started to reveal to me the offenses that my bloodline had been charged with by the enemy. I mean I was shocked at all the things that had been going on in my family. The irony of it all is that I don't know for sure what was all on my bloodline. I come from a very secretive family that sweeps things under the rug. The type of family that will take their testimonies to the grave instead of embracing their truths.

Another way to determine if there's a curse running from generation to generation is to take inventory of the family patterns. If the males in your family all die by age 21, that's a clear indicator that something in the spiritual realm is working against the family bloodline. Most people allow themselves to live in fear of what's to come from those patterns, and they feel hopeless. The problem with this mindset is that they don't consider what the solution to the problem is.

Becoming a captive to anything can range from a different set of things. As humans living in the flesh, it can be easy to allow food, money, people, alcohol, drugs, and sex to become rulers over us. Those things alone open us up to being locked into captivity. This impacts the way that we view the world and ourselves. It decreases our spiritual senses and discernment, which results in us being disconnected from hearing God & having a proper relationship with him. Many of the Generational curses we see today are related to disobedience of God's commandments and decrees. In Deuteronomy 28:41, states, "You will have sons and daughters but you will not keep them, because they will go into captivity."

While thinking about sinning and then acting upon it, you automatically place yourself on the auction block for being held captive. While God grants us grace, our greed and lust can cause repetition of behaviors that go beyond the grace he's extended to us. This is when the enemy has free range to sweep in and influence one to join the kingdom of darkness. While sinning, you begin to partner with the enemy, and that automatically makes you go against God. And that's quite the battle that you will be ill-equipped for because the enemy isn't going to equip you with weapons to defend yourself when you are a child of God! This is why you must be mindful and strategic about what, when, where, why, and how captivity takes place so that you are on the end of not getting caught up! It's important to educate yourself on what the sins are and hold yourself accountable for repenting and disciplining yourself. God gives warnings and shows his love for us with grace and mercy, but at some point, consequences are inevitable.

When you consider the idea of what being held captive can look like in different areas of your life, I want you to envision any area of life that you feel stuck in. Recall all the situations or relationships where there was rejection, abandonment, or barrenness. Some of the areas I've experienced being held captive were in my finances, friendships, family relationships, romantic relationships, business ventures, physical or mental ailments, creative ideas, and opportunities. Something that helped me break free from being held captive was through storytelling, just plainly sharing my life story. Although sharing my story is one way to set myself free, I had to keep in mind not to sin while doing so. The Bible says to honor thy father and thy mother, so before sharing my story, I had to forgive, go through therapy, and love as if they'd never hurt me. I say all of that to say I am ready to share more parts of my story; just know that it's not the easiest thing to do, but when you do hard things, ease naturally comes to you!!! The chapters in this book represent some examples of who God has been to me. He's been a true Father, friend, and much more!

### Prayer
Ask God to direct you on the sins you and your family bloodline have committed. Ask how they are impacting you today. Ask for a strategy on how to break them.

### Tip
What are three things that you'd like to partner with God on to be better at?

### Scripture
Psalms 86:11 (KJV) Teach me thy way, O LORD; I will walk in thy truth: unite my heart to fear thy name.

# Chapter Two

# Pieces of My Backstory

I'm taking off my therapist hat, role model hat, teaching hat, mom hat, and all other roles that I play in life. I have finally decided to do something for myself. I have cried many tears trying to figure out why many people haven't valued me, only to find out that it was me that was responsible for valuing me. The irony of it all is that I never took the time to consider my own needs and cater to them; I just expected other people to read my mind. I tend to think that I know what other people need, and the reality is that I do. I was gifted with an unconditional mindset and heart, and I used to think that everyone would think and act the same way I did. It was naturally easy for me to do the right thing. From a very young age, I took it upon myself to show up for others and to do the opposite of what I viewed as being wrong. The thought process took me down a long road of self-neglect, but it was necessary for me to learn that this is what made me special but also an easy target. After each heartbreak, I made a personal decision to never let that piece of me go; I knew that if I did, I would become someone who I was never meant to be. That's the power of knowing how special I am but not fully understanding who or how I was meant to show up with that gift.

    I've decided that no matter what I do in life, I will do it afraid, in the dark, while I'm yelling, kicking, and screaming if it will indeed help me to break free from any feeling of misery. After each heartbreak, I learned to reset and reevaluate my superpower of loving and nurturing others. I knew that if I kept going, I would soon discover more and more about myself and the true reality of life. From a young age, I enjoyed school and was an A+ honor roll student. It was easy for me to learn something new and apply it. I didn't require much from teachers, so I never experienced needing a tutor, and I was so quiet and shy that I never raised my hand to ask questions, and when the teachers would ask if I had any questions, I would say no. Now, I'm sure that this is why I grew into the habit of not asking questions and just leaning in on my own understanding. This is a dangerous habit when you become an adult because, for me, it created an independence that was hard to break once I decided that I needed support from others. School for me was like a walk in the park; it was swift, easy, and calming to my spirit. I enjoyed attending school because it gave me something to focus on that helped me become more curious about life. Although I didn't ask questions doesn't mean that I didn't have questions, I just didn't know or have the confidence to inquire. This is when my love for books came into play. I didn't ask anyone to provide me with books; I just figured out how to get books from the library, which eventually turned into me acquiring a load of books from the mail-in orders. I was very smart for my young age, and it could've been a magazine or a school library book from which I first ordered my book. I would fill out the mail-in order, and then the books would show up at my house in my name. I was often left at home with my siblings, so I would check the mail on my own. I don't recall there being a time that my mom asked me how or why I received the books; it was never a conversation. I was a little lady in my eyes and doing the little things that brought me joy. Books brought me joy from a young age, and they still do today, which is why I must put myself on a book budget so that I don't go overboard. When I was a kid, I would read books quickly; my favorites were mystery novels. I fell in love with Nancy Drew, alphabet mystery novels, and Goosebumps. I also enjoyed all the American Girls. These are the books that I acquired from the mail-in orders! I could write all day about my love for books, but let me tell you this, books hold great knowledge and help you to unlock parts of your brain that those around you could never teach you. Books require you to tap into your creative brain and discover things about yourself that you never could've imagined, and most importantly, they help you to learn how to spend intimate time with yourself. And that is something that I could never get enough of, ME time!

As a child, my alone time consisted of me watching my favorite cartoons and music videos. I woke up for school in the mornings to watch Care Bears, Mickey Mouse, Bobby's World, Rugrats, and Winnie the Pooh. I always had a tv in my room, but once I grew to love books, I started to watch less and less tv. I don't recall having to be told to wake up; I just had an internal alarm clock and followed a basic routine of brushing my teeth, getting dressed, styling my hair, and walking to the bus stop. I recall one picture day when my mom put my hair in a ponytail with a roller, and my only assignment for the next day was to take the roller out. When my mom received the pictures, I followed mom's instructions but didn't comb through my hair, leaving me with a perfectly rolled curl. I didn't know how I missed that step, and the fact that none of the teachers or staff tried to fix my hair made me cringe a little today. But I was in elementary school, and being responsible at a young age became an important role for me because I wanted to be an obedient child. My love for music came from my family in general; no matter if we were celebrating or not, there was music blasting through the tv or radio and in the cars whenever we were on the road. I would learn the songs and sing along as if I were performing at a concert. I would always tell myself that I would take piano lessons and sing in front of crowds one day. I had a unique gift that I kept to myself as a kid: I could make up a song and melody in my head and sing it aloud. I really sounded good but chose not to share this with others. I grew up in the habit of keeping my unique gifts to myself. I think it was God's way of helping me to develop and strengthen myself without external influences. I realized that later in life, I had internal confidence that I didn't show externally because it simply wasn't the right time. I knew in my heart that I wanted to be a role model to others, but I needed to go through a series of experiences that I am not very proud of, but it helped me to learn how to make wiser decisions. Growing requires us to take a leap of faith and do things that we've never done before. Although I did a lot of observing people, behaviors, and environments, I still was the typical curious human being who reacted off impulse and needed to feel the burn a little bit just so that I can say that I had lived and had no regrets. When I look back at the life I've lived, I do feel like I experienced all that I needed to in my younger years, and now I get to do life experiencing all the things that I thought were impossible as a young lady.

Let's do some more unplugging! I have not shown my full potential. As of today, this is something that I am continuously developing. I have all the affirmations that you can think of implanted in my head, and I'm sure you've heard of some of these and even used them yourself, "I am beautiful." "I can do anything!" "I am important." All those affirmations couldn't push me to see beyond words; I feel that life's trial and error had to teach me the true meaning of beauty, intelligence, and endless possibilities. I mean, I'd have to be silly not to take the next step forward to discover what it means to be all those things. And like the true nerd that I am, I started taking classes, watching YouTube videos, and reading books on self-development. Before 2016, you couldn't pay me to read a self-help book. I only read urban romance novels, but in 2016 I grew to love history books and documentaries.

I started diving into the Black Panther era and learning about Angela Davis and Huey P. Newton who lit a fire up under me that had me in a space of "All Black Everything" mindset. I remember that phase like it was yesterday; it helped me to start loving my blackness because, at one point as a child, I disliked my skin complexion. I grew into understanding the passion behind a revolutionary person, and I always had a passion for rebelling against morally wrong things, such as racism and discrimination against women. I had my fair share of issues I had experienced from childhood to the present. Reading these books helped me to normalize all the things that God had been showing me about myself from a little girl, and it put more things about my childhood into perspective. Like, the bullying and not knowing how to speak up for me. I decided as an adult that I wouldn't take any mess from a person trying to verbally or physically harm myself or anyone around me, including the people I worked with. I later learned that was a heavy burden to place upon myself because while I was trying to save other people from being harmed, I received a rejection. I once read a statement that said, "Before you try to save a person, ask them if they want to be saved." That statement will forever stick with me because I was the person who always tried to rescue people until I realized that others would not consciously do the same for me. I've been burned more times than I'd like to admit; having a good heart isn't always a good thing. You must learn how to use it without trying to manipulate others into loving you or giving you attention.

## Prayer

Ask God to show you how certain life experiences have shaped your view today.

## Tip

What are five things that you believe about God?

## Scripture

Psalms 25:5 (KJV) Lead me in thy truth, and teach me: for thou art the God of my salvation; on thee do I wait all the day.

## Chapter Three

# God is the Truth, Be True to You

I've often heard that for one to be true to oneself, one must know what that entails. I can honestly say that it took experience after experience for me to fully understand what my truth looked like. I always had the idea in the back of my head, but the fruit of how I showed up in life showed me otherwise. I often would tell myself, "I'm working on getting myself together." "I'm going to get better and better as I age." This is how I would honestly motivate myself, but it was also a way to escape the realities of life. My way of self-motivation was to keep experiencing whatever heartbreak, pain, and failures that I needed to so that I would gain more understanding of what I was doing wrong so that I could learn how to do it right. I learned this as a child. I would see family, peers, and other people making poor decisions, and I would say to myself, "welp, if that's the result, then I will not do what they did." That resulted in my living life that way, but it wasn't helpful because even though I saw it done the wrong way didn't automatically put me at the forefront of doing things the right way. It was just an option scratched off the list of multiple ways that people do things and end up with the same results. Because guess what? I truly ended up with the same results as the family, peers, and people I had made a vow not to be like. I learned the art of fabrication and making something that's ugly on the inside look beautiful outside. I now recognize that what I did was put a mask over the reality of who I was, which resulted in me having unfavorable relationships. I always tell people, "Show who you are upfront so that you give people the opportunity to see the real you." That quote came from me being a master at people pleasing while trying to get people to stay in my life. Do you see how damaging abandonment impacts a person over time? I was way over my head when I started people-pleasing in friendships. I would offer to pick people up, pay for things, and give wise counsel, but I never took a step back to see what they had to offer me or even what my friend's needs were. The more depleted I felt in the friendship, the more I would do. Being a servant to others has always been a fulfilling task for me. It makes me feel happy to show up and give something that I must give to another. My problem was that I ended up being more of a people pleaser than a servant. A people pleaser invests in another person with the expectation that they will gain favor from that person. Servants show up to serve with the expectation that they are helping a person in need and that they do not expect a return. There's a huge difference between the two, and it often led me to a corner crying about a failed friendship and back into the arms of unhealthy family relationships. I was what you'd call a chronic forgiver; I'd go back to people who once betrayed me with the idea that since time has passed, surely, they have learned their lesson. Unbeknownst to me, I had learned the art of ignoring red flags. At some point in my life, there were red lights, big and bright red with a stop sign.

God is a way maker and the truth. He does not lie or deceive others, but the enemy does. The enemy of our minds, bodies, spirits, and souls can turn us away from God when we don't understand who God is and how he operates. Deception looks different depending on the calling one has in their life. For me, deception came through relationships, how I spent money, the food that I ate, confusing decisions, and how I reviewed myself. In relationships, deception showed up with me attracting people who represented a false identity. It would typically take 3-6 months before the reality of the person started to shine through. I feel like when people came into my life, I had these rose-colored glasses on; everything appeared to be bright, fun, and beautiful. Somewhere along the way, their behaviors would change, and my flesh would have this desperate need for them to the point that I was willing to look past major flaws. If you've ever been that person to say, "I would never allow that in a relationship," then you know what I mean. I was allowing individuals to offend me in ways that I didn't speak to myself or would speak to others. There were actions being taken by others that I would never think of doing to another person. But I would excuse the behavior and actions towards me until it was no longer excusable. When you don't know your worth or value and have never had anyone explain or role model what it should look like to value yourself, you must figure it out yourself.

The beauty in having a relationship with God is that he does the educating for you. Anything that you didn't acquire from your parents, he supplies your every need. I leaned in on him more after I ignored his warnings within relationships. He was guiding me on what to do and say the entire time; I was just too naive to listen. The deception came from being desperate. When you want to feel loved to the point that you will accept things that are non-negotiable, you become absent from the body and lost in your emotions. The fact that we don't see emotions unless it's acted out through behavior is one thing, but to be lost in an emotion that allows you to detach from reality is dangerous. God didn't design us to have this kind of suffering. This kind comes from disobedience, idolatry, and all the other sins. I learned a valuable lesson from these experiences. Be true to what your first mind tells you to do. If your mind tells you no, then the response and behavior need to be in alignment with it. It doesn't matter if the no will create conflict, ask yourself, "Is it more important to maintain peace within or externally?" I can guarantee you that when you maintain the peace within, life gets easier, and your relationships get better!

But we all fall short in life; it's not about the decisions that we have made that led us to the fall but how we respond to the fall. I recall falling into lust, believing it was love and being attracted to things from a place of desperation. Neither of those things makes me feel good when I look back at the memories. There was a time when I had a group of friends that I had grown a connection with during my high school years. One friend I had fallen out of friendship with during my middle school years but reconnected with in high school. There were also a few other people I had surface-level relationships with but reconnected with in high school. When I think about those friendships, I never had a consistent 1:1 or group of friends that lasted for more than a school year prior to high school. I was able to show up and be myself and not get lost in a crowd of folks like many tend to do. I enjoyed having more solo friendships because sharing pieces of myself with others was a lot of work, and it appeared to me that others' problems were always bigger than mine, or that's what I told myself. I was naturally a counselor at a young age. I would listen to my friends' advice and give them encouragement. I don't recall sharing much about myself because it was easy for me to minimize my own problems, but also, I had grown accustomed to keeping things inside. The beauty of building a relationship with God and trusting him is that I was able to relinquish that habit and be vulnerable through the good, bad, and ugly. Being held captive wasn't just something that the enemy was doing to me; it was something that I had learned to do to myself. See how tricky life can be? The enemy puts an idea in your mind, and before you know it, you are duplicating it in different areas of your life. I have fallen short because of not having spiritual discernment.

I like to view myself as a loyal friend, but when I consider who those individuals grew up to be, I can see why they didn't remain in my life. See, back then, the Lord was giving me specific instructions on who to be friends with and who to let go of, but I was too blind to see. I was only looking at things from a surface level and only from the point of view of what I did wrong. I had never seen a healthy friendship growing up, so the friendships that I did acquire meant a lot to me. I now know when to listen to God telling me who should and shouldn't be in my life and accept when a person's time has come to an end in my life.

### Prayer
Thank God for being a way maker, a protector, a leader, and whoever else he has been to you.

### Tip
In what ways have you been disobedient? What are you doing now to be obedient?

### Scripture
Psalms 106:1 (KJV) Praise ye the LORD. O give thanks unto the LORD; for he is good: for his mercy endureth for ever.

## Chapter Four

# God's Grace is Sufficient

When I reflect on my past, I realize that growing up, I was given a lot of second-hand knowledge and, in most cases, information that was passed down from generation to generation. If you've even told a person one thing and their interpretation left information out, you'll understand where I'm going. Well, as a kid, I was taught that going to church was important, but I wasn't given instructions on the importance of attending or how I should live outside of the church. I was told that it was inappropriate to fall asleep while in church service. I should always pray and attend service weekly. I don't have any memories of people teaching me how to pray or what I should pray for, so I always led with "God is good, God is great, let us thank him for our food today. Or "Now I lay me down to sleep, I pray the Lord, my soul, to keep and if I die before I wake, I pray the Lord my soul to take." These are simple, sweet prayers that I know are great starters for all children. Oh, and I must not forget to pray for the people I love! So, I did this for years, until my adult life, because it was the beginning and the end of my teachings about the church. I grew up in a household that praised God but didn't attend church. I do not recall one moment of going to church with my mother outside of attending funerals. My father never spoke about God or went to church, from my understanding. My earliest memories about church came from my godmother, Shirley. I would stay with her for the weekend and fall asleep listening to church music or Boys II Men. We would dress up for church and go through the usual steps of Sunday school and sit in church all day, literally all day. I sat with my godmother most of the time and remembered the Preacher shouting and jumping down the aisle. The choir and hearing the preacher yelling were the two things that would keep me awake. Honestly, my godmother played music so loud that I woke up a lot singing along to the music. This is one recurring event that interfered with my later years of issues with sleeping as an adult. Church, for me, was an escape; it made me feel good and forget about all the pain that I had endured during the week. Over time I started to view the church as a reset only I could obtain in the house of the Lord. In my later years, I learned that I could take the church with me everywhere I went, even in my own home. Church as a kid also looked like me, my sister, and cousins walking to a local church in our neighborhood, still no parents in tow. The church we would attend on our own was much different from the Baptist church that my godmother attended. This church had a white pastor, and while it was a culture shock, I felt comfortable and welcomed attending it. The church was different because it was a quick service and didn't have as much shouting, yelling, and dancing, so it was always an easy in-and-out service that helped us kids have time to play in the neighborhood. I only recall attending that church a few times. As I'm aging, and I'm only in my 30s, I'm starting to forget many memories that I feel would be beneficial for me to reflect on.

Although many have experienced church hurt, that was never my own personal experience. I didn't get the opportunity to build a relationship with a pastor, First Lady, or anyone in the church. My mother would often speak about the pain she endured in the church but would never go into details. As I met people along my journey of self-discovery, I encountered several people who spoke about the abuse they endured from the church. Their trauma experience led them to label their experience as being the standard for all churches. I knew that it couldn't be the case because people are the ones who make poor decisions to lead the church in an ungodly manner. I knew that it was not God's original design for abuse to take place in the church, so I never blamed the church for the error of a human. Hearing others' stories demotivated me to believe that I needed a church home.

I mean, I didn't want to experience anything like I had heard before. I had many failed relationships with people in general that kept me on guard from meeting new people, especially those in the church.

While reading the Bible and listening to sermons, my heart started to shift to God's original design for the church, his ecclesia. I craved an understanding that would help me make a wise choice on the church I would choose to step into. I didn't want to rush the process, but I knew God was leading me to be in the church. Hearing him give me the desire to join a church automatically made me immediately agree. I've learned a few things about obedience. It's better to agree with God's plans the first time around than to disagree and end up with delays that will lead you back around to the same instruction. I believe that if you haven't told God no to his plan, then he never really gave you a plan. His plans are so big that they don't make sense to us originally! While reading the Bible, I understood that there were many benefits to going to church, such as building a community. The church is meant to accept those who are seeking God. The church should display Christ-like behaviors and attitudes so that people can see the fruit and benefits of having a relationship with God. For those who don't have a family, the church is where you learn how a healthy family is supposed to operate. When you are down, the church guides you on how to stay faithful throughout the storm and how to commune with people to maintain a posture of peace and victory. The church is also the place where you worship and give praise to God for who he is. This is one of my favorite things to do. The body of Christ being all on one accord through praise and worship is an experience like no other! I didn't know I had it within me to praise for hours until I was sitting in a crowd of people who love Jesus and were unapologetic with their shouts and praises. I used to sit in church and lack understanding of how people could be so loud. I used to think to myself, "It's not that deep." But the real problem was that I wasn't that deep and that I was cheating myself from the experience of that same loud and beautiful sound. The funny thing is, I used to go to the club and be the first and last one on the dance floor, reciting all the words to all kinds of ungodly music. The way that I used to shout and dance was the way that I should've always been doing for the Lord. I thank God for changing my ways. When the Bible says, "My people perish for lack of knowledge," it was speaking about me and all the times I was ignorant of beliefs and habits. The time that I spent in the club opened many demonic doors that God had to deliver me from. There are times that I recall drinking, flirting, and lusting excessively to the point that I'd be open to one-night stands. The fact that I wouldn't desire that while I was sober says a lot. While I wasn't leaving the club with men, there was this strange urge for me to so I would make it as far as giving out my number to multiple people by the end of the night. For a foolish reason, that was an accomplishment. I was searching for and desiring love so badly that I was overly flirtatious, thinking it would get a man's attention. I realized that the only attention I was receiving was from men who were ready to take advantage of me. But God protected me on many occasions. I'd wake up the next day from a text from the person, and by the end of the day, and sometimes that week, they ghosted me. This happened a lot to the point that I was used to rejection. I used to say to myself that the person must've been intoxicated, and once they sobered up and realized how I looked, they changed their mind. That, to me, was better than thinking about anything else. It was a painful thought, but all along, God was protecting me. He knew the spirit behind those individuals, and he knew the plans that he had for me. While I was focused on feeding my flesh, he was teaching me the art of dying in the flesh, which is the true death we all need when building a relationship with him. We need to understand that our flesh can be deceiving, and it will lead us onto a destructive path. A path that can be long and dark. I thank God for cutting that path for me short! I know that he is a miracle worker because of the way that the enemy had my mind; I had no idea the way that I was living was wrong.

Over the last several years, I've worked on shedding several layers of trauma. Trauma that we will get to later in the book. My desire is to recall all those small, sweet, and innocent memories by the time I finish writing this book. The purpose of that is to allow my brain to fully accept the healing and the new journey that I am embarking on. I'd love to make space for new memories and shed myself on the painful ones.

## Prayer

Thank God for molding, shaping, and developing you into who he desires you to be. Ask for strength to not focus on others' lives but on your relationship with him.

## Tip

Reflect on all the changes God has brought you through in your life. Build confidence knowing that he will continue carrying you.

## Scripture

Psalms 16:8 (KJV) I have set the LORD always before me: because he is at my right hand, I shall not be moved.

## Chapter Five

# God is a Healer

I have had many low points in my life where I just had no desire to live. The earliest age I can recall feeling this way was 12 years ago. By that age, I had encountered more than a handful and felt like if this was what the world had to offer me, then it wasn't worth it. One outlet that I picked up on as a 12-year-old was writing. I have continued to adapt writing as a coping skill today.

Believe it or not, 2022 was one of the worst years of my life. I cried so many tears and stayed on my knees praying to Christ. I felt like I was suffocating from my ancestors' decisions, but a few years back, I was unconsciously praising my ancestors' decisions. 2022 is also the year I came into new knowledge that helped me gain an understanding of idolatry. Then the veil dropped from over my eyes, and I was able to see things so clearly. 35

years of pain, and I haven't uncovered it all. Even the things I've discovered almost made me want to lose it all. God showed me the importance of letting go and then led me on a path of shedding. I had to shed everything I once knew and even the new things I thought I knew just to really see the truth.

The truth was the ugliest thing I had ever endured. Have you ever bit into a sandwich that you were craving only to find out that the bread was molded, and you had an instant loss of appetite? That's how I came into a new awareness about the depths of my bloodline. A few years back, I received a message from the Holy Spirit about being the chosen one, and oh man, was I in for a surprise. Now if you know me, I am a nerd. I love to learn, and I don't stop at just learning one thing; I keep diving in deeper. This is what led me to where I am today. While it came with many restless nights and fearful moments, I am grateful because now I have an extra layer of faith and clarity regarding my purpose. It all started in 2019 when I started getting an itch to go to church. Then I picked up the Psalms and was so intrigued by the prayers that I started focusing on asking God to increase my knowledge, understanding, and wisdom. Even as I type this, I am shocked that I really prayed for this while not understanding what I was getting myself into. Now to know me is to know that I'm always putting myself into situations that I didn't inquire the full details about before agreeing to it.

I recall back in 2011, I visited Colorado once, and a friend at the time encouraged me to relocate there. I went along with it because I wanted to leave my hometown to escape the deep depression I had been experiencing, and I also had big dreams that I knew I needed to go to another state to accomplish. Colorado was the cleanest and most beautiful place I had visited. I was accustomed to visiting the small southern cities that had only a few thousand people, so I hadn't experienced what it looked like to be in a city where people looked healthy and wealthy. Soon after visiting, I applied to a college there, got accepted with a scholarship, and moved there within a span of 6 months. It's a long story behind that, but what I wasn't prepared for was moving from a city of 100,000+ people to 633,000+, with higher prices for everything while only making less than $12 an hour. Then on top of that, I didn't research how much tuition would cost because I was so wrapped up in obtaining a scholarship that I didn't inquire about the full tuition until I was already locked in. I was under the impression that it was covered, not realizing that I had applied for a private school in Colorado, of all places! Talk about a huge mess I had put myself into. But I look back on everything and know that if I had researched everything before relocating, I wouldn't have gone because I would have talked myself into thinking that I couldn't do it and that it was impossible for me to relocate under those specific circumstances. I was a reasonable person when it came to finances and making sure that I had the income to cover my basic needs. Relocating without knowing what I got myself into pushed me into a hustle mode that I didn't know I had because once I got to Colorado, my focus was never to return to my hometown. I knew what to expect back home because I had been there for 24 years, and it wasn't anything good for me to build on. So, I stayed to make it work, and guess what? God had his hands on me the entire time because I still couldn't tell you how I made it, but I'm glad I did!

As you can see, making decisions while discerning the situation wasn't my strongest ability. But towards the end of 2022, I asked God to increase my discernment, and oh yes, he did it immediately and expeditiously. My head started to spin at all the information that the Holy Spirit was downloading into my brain. If you've ever received a revelation, you'll understand what I mean! The information came like an unwanted neighbor knocking at my door, and I had no choice but to see and respond. My immediate thought was wow, I'm grateful for this information. Then when I realized what I had to do, I was instantly hit with grief. Grief, because I had to make a big decision to let something go that I had no idea, was a hindrance to my growth. Also, it played a huge part in my mental well-being. My intuition was telling me all along that it wasn't healthy, but my heart just wouldn't let up. My heart was fabricating the ugly truth. Now, I've been known to make something ugly sound small and manageable. But this was a situation that I just couldn't play with. I mean, I was tossing and turning for over a week, feeling the shift take place. Then I decided that I wanted to sleep, and I mean sleep like a baby. I then did the hardest thing I've ever had to do; I said no. I mean, I said no to the sleepless nights, taking on extra burdens, being lied to, manipulated, and taken for granted. I was proud of myself for doing that, but it was short-lived because my heart kept getting in the way. So, then I started losing sleep because my heart and mind were in a tug-of-war battle. While my mind was fighting the flesh, my heart was willing to take another miscalculated risk down the heartbreak lane.

God healed me on many different levels. I recall a time in my life when I was taking five medications. I had asthma, environmental allergies, acid reflux, and anxiety. These combinations of medications made me feel like I was drowning and in a never-ending cycle. I was too young to take that many medications, plus it was for very minor issues. I did not know what to do about the medications, but I had a strong belief that I could live without them; I just needed to find a way to do so. That level of faith was something that I had unknowingly, meaning that I didn't include God in this plan.

When I look back at that time in my life, I'm pretty sure that God was the one who gave me the idea. The beautiful thing about God is that he doesn't need our permission to do anything. He has set many of us apart to fulfill his plans for his people. I believe that God snatched me up on several occasions and pushed me into my destiny because had he not, I would've been led down a path of destruction. He did it in such a strategic way that I had no choice but to ever doubt that it was him. While I was living as if I had no one in the world, God was right in front of me, making my crooked paths straight. When I say he is a healer, he led me into a healthier way of eating, thinking and being so that I could rid myself of the medications I was on. The faith I had in being certain that I didn't need the medications led me closer to him. Back then, I acknowledged him as a "Higher Power" because I didn't know if I was comfortable calling him God. While I was in a life transition of discovering myself and beliefs, he never changed.

The way that he healed me and protected me was the same way that he did when I had a relationship with him before straying away for 7 years. I always tell myself that it must've been the prayers from my grandmother that kept me all along. I often forget that I had a relationship with him from a young age and was diligently trying to seek him all but those 7 years that I went astray. Maybe the little 4, 13, 19-year-old planted seeds that led me to where I am with him today. I'm going to choose to believe that it was many layers, but also, God chose me to fulfill a specific purpose, and everything happened in the timing that he originally designed for me. This is why I love the scripture, "For I know the thoughts that I think toward you, saith the LORD, thoughts of peace, and not of evil, to give you an expected end."

God knew all along that I'd make foolish decisions, but he knew exactly what my heart needed to repent and turn back to him. Turning to him gave me a sense of comfort, understanding, and appreciation for him more than ever before. He loved me enough to come back for me and had patience that I could never understand. His mercy and grace are everything to me! When he healed my heart in 2022, he also gave me the position of Sunday school teacher. I had never given a Bible lesson other than what I shared with my son by this time. I started to pray and ask God to help guide me along the way. He showed up more than I could've asked for, and the feedback from the students and others was amazing. In 2021, he gave me a prophetic dream of being in my hometown and teaching a group of students. I reflected on the dream initially and thought I'd be a substitute teacher. Guess what I did with the prophecy of me moving back to my hometown? I applied to be a substitute teacher at a private school. I was so excited that I was accepted for the position. I was working full time in my business at the time, but I was willing to take a lower pay a few days a month to pour into teens. I've always had a love for youth and a desire to be a good role model. I waited months for a call to serve as a substitute teacher, and guess what? It never came. I was a little sad but grateful that I took the chance to be willing to serve. While I was going through all that I was in 2022, I still had a desire to give back in any way that I could. I received a call later in the school year to substitute, but by this time, I was busy volunteering with the church and deeper into my Bible studying sessions and speaking the word on my YouTube channel. Within a matter of months, I had gained a surge of enthusiasm to share the good news, which was so amazing. God saw something in me that it took years for me to see in myself. While I am still getting used to who he's calling me to be, I'm slowly getting better at acknowledging it all. I never could've imagined that this was where I'd be in life, loving God, and all it took was for me to listen and be obedient. He is an awesome healer.

**Prayer**
Ask for spiritual discernment to make wise choices.

**Tip**
Evaluate your life to see if you have been idolizing anything other than God. Then plan to repent and turn away from the behavior. Then renounce every curse and evil covenant that you agreed to while participating in the sin.

**Scripture**
1 John 4:1 (KJV) Beloved, believe not every spirit, but try the spirits whether they are of God: because many false prophets are gone out into the world.

## Chapter Six

# He Brings Peace

I believe that throughout our life, we go through a phase of resurrection, where we let go of old ways of thinking, being, and existing. I have had over five major transitions in life, and I am currently embarking upon the most powerful one yet to date. There has been a transition of belief systems that I've explored based on what I found when I was more worldly than Christian. After relocating to Colorado, I discovered what it meant to be seen and desired by others. But it's also a time that showed me that just because people are seeing you doesn't mean that they are present for you. I moved there with a dollar and a dream; no, literally, I used all my tax money to move there and didn't have a job lined up. I had a bachelor's degree and was a certified nursing assistant, so I figured it wouldn't be hard to find employment with those skills. I had always been a good steward of the jobs I acquired and made sure that I always left in good standing. I was confident in finding a job, but I was also basing my decision while coming out of a deep depression. You see, I have been battling with depression since the age of 11, but I knew how to hide it because I wanted to work my way away from it. Did it help? No, but I have always been determined not to let a person, situation, or feeling weigh me down or keep me from chasing my dreams. I always felt that the depression was situational and that I'd eventually bounce back and forget about the former things that led me to the darkness. But the truth is, I was selling myself a dream just to get by, which I did during all those moments of darkness. I learned that I could at least be the light for others, which honestly brought a sense of happiness. But it came to a point where I was so deep in that I couldn't even fake it; that's when I flunked out of graduate school. I remember working two jobs and feeling drained after a breakup that I started to not care about school. I didn't complete schoolwork, and when I did, I failed the assignments. My mind was all over the place, and before it got too bad, I decided to drop the classes before an actual F showed up on my transcripts. I may not have been in my right mind during that time, but I sure knew that after I snapped out of it, I'd need my good GPA to rely on. The way that I looked on paper meant a lot to me and failing let me know that I absolutely had to let certain people out of my life. Each time I look back on life, I find that I was equipped with wisdom while in the midst of a whole mental hurricane.

My first hurricane came around the age of six when I witnessed my mother stab her boyfriend. I remember it like it was yesterday, my mom often hosted family and friends at our home, but she and her boyfriend also had a lot of verbal and physical fights. So, this night was a typical night except for the vivid flashback that I have of seeing her friend pass her a large kitchen knife. I don't recall what they were arguing about, all I saw next was blood gushing out of his back, and then the ambulance was called and hauled him away. I don't remember if the police were called, but I'm sure they were. As a kid, I felt that whatever the situation was, he would be gone forever because that's what happens when a person is stabbed, right? Well, he and my mom ended up getting right back together; I think he was back in the house the next day. I was sure hoping that he wouldn't return because I didn't like him one bit. As a child, I had great discernment, but growing up in a black household where trauma was common and things were swept under the rug, kids ignored when expressing to other adults that a person made them feel uncomfortable. I often look back at my 20s and wish I had the discernment I had as a child, but it faded due to being ignored. After that stabbing incident, I went through many more violent episodes until I reached the age of 12 when they finally decided to depart. There was another stabbing and many physical fights, some of which I jumped in the middle of to stop. I was never physically harmed, but I called the cops on many occasions. The cops were at our house every week to the point that one day the cop told my mom she needed to leave him before she ended up dead. That statement alone hurt to the core that I started to yell at the cop, but what he had said was true; it was just sad that my mother couldn't see it for herself. I was close to my mom growing up, and I always had her back, and when anyone would talk about her, I'd be ready to write them off. I was a loyal daughter because I felt that my mom would do it for me until I realized she never made decisions to keep me safe because I was always in a constant state of fear.

In my early 20's, I encountered a valuable lesson that taught me the importance of "mind my own business." I was in a phase in life where I was passionate about people and strong about seeking justice. I was in a state of "I will help everyone that I can." The first ministry I felt was important to help was family, so I did whatever I could, whether it be showing up to help them problem solve, protecting them from emotional or physical abuse, or just helping financially. There was a situation where my mother was dating a guy, and I decided to accept that she wanted to be with him despite it being obvious that they weren't a good fit for each other. I attended celebrations and family gatherings and would be respectful of the person she dated. Then they got married, and once they broke up, which happened within less than a year. Then there was a situation that I guess I just couldn't stay out of. To make a long story short, I decided I wanted justice for how he had been treating my mother after the breakup. I was in a state of rage over the information I had heard from my mother's friend that I had decided it was necessary to defend my mother. Within a matter of 1-2 days after learning about the incident, I saw him while walking through a movie theater. My mind instantly went into a rage, and I blacked out. During the blackout, as vividly as I can recall, I started to swing with a closed fist into his face. The rage was so intense that I felt like I flew over to the other side of the room, and before I knew it, my sister was pulling me away from him. Now, me fighting in public was not a typical thing; as a matter of fact, this wasn't like me at all to cause such a ruckus at a movie theater that was jam-packed! I left the scene immediately and drove off, but I was in a stage of rage for a few days until I calmed down. Later in the month, I received a court notice that I was being requested for a court hearing due to accusations of "mob action." The entire document spewed false information about all the parties involved. However, it was only me, but my sister's name was mentioned, so we both had to attend court. I was completely confused during the process as the court-appointed lawyer assigned to us told us that we should just plead guilty because they had witnesses. Now, keep in mind we left before the police arrived, so none of the witnesses knew me nor my sister, but we were scared, so we pled guilty. During the court hearing, my mother was there with us. She said something very shocking to me that taught me a valuable lesson. She said, "That's what you get; you shouldn't have been trying to fight him in the first place." Then she proceeded to laugh. I didn't think anything was funny because I was being fined for something that I did to defend her. But this led me to evaluate my behavior. Yes, it was wrong because, at the end of the day, I should've kept my hands to myself, and wrong is wrong. That day taught me that just because I love someone doesn't mean that I need to pick up their burdens and try to fix their problems for them. It was at that moment that I decided that I would keep my hands to myself and I would focus on myself and my son only. Also, I learned the importance of being a better manager of my emotions and how I didn't want to carry on in life, operating from the idea that fighting was ok.

Later in life, I began to understand how God removed me from people, environments, and situations that would bring me to a state of rage. He knew my family's fighting history and didn't want me to carry out the same generational habits. He needed me to be far away from the things that triggered me. I had to build a relationship with him to learn how to better manage my emotions and how I fought or sought out justice. He taught me the art of fasting and praying, and I now know how to war in the spiritual realm, the proper way, which has brought me much peace mentally, physically, and spiritually!

### Prayer
Ask God to bring you peace in any area of your life that's not within your control.

### Tip
Reflect on everything that's within your control in life and evaluate how you're managing those things.

### Scripture
John 14:27 (KJV) "Peace I leave with you, my peace I give unto you: not as the world giveth, give I unto you. Let not your heart be troubled, neither let it be afraid."

## Chapter Seven

# He is a Great Provider & Deliverer

I was under the age of ten when I first started to watch porn. Yes, we are diving deep right away because it is better to just rip the band-aid off to start the healing. If you felt conviction reading that, then imagine how I feel writing this for people to read. I've come to an understanding that my truth is my truth, and if I don't stand up and speak it, someone may try to tell my story for me, or others may falsely perceive it. See, most of my life, I hid behind life experiences and showed up in the world presenting as if I was flawed, without error. That was never my intention; it was just a protective guard that I put up at a young age. When you start doing things as a kid, you won't grow out of it until you are told that you're doing something wrong. I wasn't paid much attention to so the perspectives and habits I started as a kid grew with me because I didn't share, and no one asked. I remember telling adults something one time, and they didn't do anything about it, so I made it a point to not speak up if it was going to be pointless. I had the attitude of "Fine, I'll figure it out on my own." When I look back at that now, I can see why adulthood was so challenging for me. It created a narrative for others that I didn't need their help and that they were useless in my life. That was far from the truth. I needed people to support me, show up for me, listen to me, and affirm me. It resulted in me not knowing how to tell people what I needed; instead, I did all those things for others until I became burned out. And oh, the burnout was cycle after cycle in romantic relationships.

My experience with porn had my mind confused, and lust swept across me, creating this curiosity about what it would be like to perform those acts with a guy. I never tried to allow any boys my age to touch me because I felt that it would give off the wrong impression of me, so I would find activities to do to soothe the discomfort I felt with lust. I didn't fully understand the concept of sex, so I didn't explore my body until I became an adult. When I look back at that, I am thankful because things could've been worse. At a young age, I was under the impression that I needed to keep my body pure, and I may have learned that in church and seeing my family having kids left and right may have also caused me not to be too curious. Growing up, there were several incidents that I can recall where I was desired by older men. It was the looks from them. I recall a time when I was in middle school, walking down the street, and a guy almost broke his neck driving down the street, staring at me. That made me very uncomfortable as I knew it was wrong to be looked at sexually. The earliest incident that I recall of sexual exploitation occurred when I was 7/8 years old. I was just being a typical kid in my home on a day off from school, or it could've been the summertime while my mom was at work. I was walking to use the bathroom across the hall from my bedroom. Before I would get to the bathroom, my mother's bedroom was on the left side, heading straight into the bathroom. When I look back at the memories in that house, it makes me thankful that God protected me. This is the same house where the stabbings took place. The size of the house was a small, three-bedroom home. As I was walking towards the bathroom, I heard my mom's boyfriend call my name. When I looked up, I saw their bedroom door wide open, him standing up in the bedroom, fully naked and stroking his penis. I immediately ran back to my room in fear. But I really needed to use the bathroom, so I had to think quickly so that I didn't pee on myself. I grabbed my little brother, 1-2 years old and walking, who was his son and had my brother walk to the left side, closer to their bedroom. I held my brother's hand tight as I was in complete fear of what could happen to me. I kept looking straight and wouldn't let my eyes fall into any other direction other than the bathroom. Once I got into the bathroom, I let my brother go, leaving him in the hallway, then I shut and locked the bathroom door. When I was finished with the bathroom, I was afraid of what I was going to walk into after I was finished. So again, I had to think quickly about what I was going to do. Instantly I opened the door, ran to my bedroom, and shut the door! I only recall this situation happening once, but I was filled with anger for many years. I couldn't understand why we had to live in a household with a pervert. The man was mean, a drug addict, a pervert, and overall, I didn't like him! He was never liked by many people in my family, and my mother was always working while he was in the house, being a pervert, selling drugs, and playing video games.

I felt unsafe around men from that day forward and didn't trust them, especially after I decided to tell the truth a year or so later. I was called a liar, and nothing was done about it. I lived in a home with the perpetrator for 6+ years after that. While we moved from home to home during my elementary school years, I started picking up my passion for writing. In the 4th grade, I won a young authors award for a book that I wrote about dinosaurs. I loved the stegosaurus! While I was flourishing in school, receiving all A's, it was becoming more and more dreadful for me to live in our home. The violence didn't stop, and I was forever fearful that my mom's boyfriend would try the perverted act again. It was hard to shake the thought out of my mind, so I picked up a few habits to keep me in control of the fear. I journaled, wrote songs, listened to a lot of music, read my Bible, and daydreamed. I once wrote a rap with all kinds of vulgar lyrics in it, along with what happened with my mom's boyfriend. I took the notebook with me whenever I went because sometime prior to me using a notebook, my mom's boyfriend was sneaking into my bedroom while I was at school reading my diary. The diary was locked, but he would find it, and it would be obvious he had read it because it would be sitting on my bed instead of under my mattress, where I kept it when I returned home from school. So, when I say I was fearful, that's an understatement. I didn't know how to communicate my feelings, needs, likes/dislikes, and I couldn't even have the privacy to do it all without someone intruding into my life. One weekend while staying over at my dad's house, I took the notebook with me. My dad must've been cleaning up, saw the notebook, and read it. I recall him being angry about the incident, which I finally decided to share with him. I also shared how hard living with my mom was because of her boyfriend. I found some comfort in sharing and was hopeful that life would change now that I no longer had to carry this burden. Because of how angry my dad was, I was certain that he would move me and my sister out of the home. What happened that day was expected; what came about afterwards was unexpected. My father went to my mother's home and had a verbal argument and possibly a physical altercation with her boyfriend. The truth is, I was expecting the fight because I had seen them have verbal and physical fights quite a bit in my life prior to this situation, and it wasn't the last one. Now I was 100% sure that because of how my dad reacted, he would pull me out of the home and have me live with him. The complete opposite happened; everything was complete crickets on my dad's end. There are many memories that I can recall, but I recall nothing but life as usual for all involved adults from that dad forward. Eventually, anger grew on the inside of me, more fear was present, and I knew from that day forward I could not trust the people who brought me into the world and definitely not the people that were in their lives. I made a vow to never allow myself to be hurt and controlled to the point that I'd lose my integrity for the sake of love. I also started to plan my exit for the future; I took observations of how everyone around me was living and made a vow not to make the same mistakes. I was a baby making these vows, Bhutto; since I didn't have anyone to talk to, I kept it to myself. I never thought to share these experiences at school because I enjoyed class, having a friend or two, and being a happy person. I didn't want to bring any negativity into school because I was already afraid of how others would see me. But I kept my Bible close and leaned on the promises of God, "He will never leave me."

During my late elementary, middle school, and early high school days, I didn't watch porn, but I had many friends who were sexually active and would tell me their stories. Hearing their stories didn't make me curious, it made me disgusted that they'd be sharing their bodies and doing sexual acts with others in the school bathrooms. At that phase in my life, I dressed like a tomboy but was a nerd. I didn't want any boys looking at my body; I had enough sexual looks from men to keep my mind off that. I was focused on school and making it out of the home I lived in. I ultimately wanted peace, and learning brought me just that. I may not have been watching porn, but there were overly sexual music videos I'd watch on BET uncut. As I look back, I recognize just how I wasn't monitored, and it left me with too much time on my hands to explore. That was the beginning of sexual perversion that lasted into my early 30s. It had such a strong hold over me that I thought I needed a romantic partner to have sex with, so I kept a person around, no matter if I had broken up with them or not, just to satisfy my sexual needs. Then God shifted the scenario, and then I had access to no one. It seemed like they started to drop out of my life, left and right with no explanation. When I look back at it, I know that it was God protecting me because the behavior could've gotten out of hand. The older I got and the more stressed in life I became, the more I'd desire sex and the more I craved marriage. However, this was the start of God purging me from all the things taking root in my life and creating a gap between him and me. I grew to understand his plans for me and the errors in my ways that stopped me from marriage. I was in disbelief after watching Tony Gaskin speak on a YouTube video about women staying off their backs, meaning to stop having sex while unmarried. It was at that moment that I stopped craving a man to fulfill my sexual needs and decided that it was time for me to unlearn some behaviors and find a healthy way to discipline myself.

 I came to an agreement with it, but the porn addiction stopped later, not right away. I talked myself into cutting back on porn because I had gotten out of control with it then I recognized that I was still in the wrong for it because I would feel guilty whenever I'd listen to a video on abstinence and how masturbation was connected to abstinence. It was a hard pill to swallow, so I'd pull back more and more until I decided to do a 30-day detox from it. During that time, it was easy because I had a lot of stressors in my life and turned to working out and working more to curb the urges. I set up a daily routine and followed it with no relapses. The problem was that once my 30 days were up, I jumped back into it, but it was different that time around. I was doing it every 2 weeks, which was much less than I've ever done. I figured that was better than what I did before, so I kept disciplining myself. At this point, my body and mind were telling me I needed to do it, but I'd tell myself no. I eventually got to the point where I fasted and told God to shed me of everything that was meant to break me and steal my identity at a young age. That very moment is when I understood how the experiences from childhood distorted my perspective of sex. I started to read the bible and talk with God about some of his plans for me. I then vowed to be obedient, and it felt good. I instantly started to see great things happening in my life that confirmed that God was on my side and that I no longer needed to fulfill a broken piece of myself. I was whole at that moment. And that gave me the peace I had been searching for since I was a kid. That peace that only comes with obedience!

## Prayer

Thank God for delivering you from strongholds placed on you by the enemy.

## Tip

Identify what triggers the strongholds and how you will maintain your deliverance.

## Scripture

1 John 4:4 (KJV) Ye are of God, little children, and have overcome them: because greater is he that is in you, than he that is in the world.

## Chapter Eight

# Get to Know Jesus; He is Victorious!

Between the ages of 10-12, I started to crave a closer relationship with God. I had two Bibles, one large and a small, orange Bible, that I would carry in my purse. I owned several purse-sized copies throughout my lifetime, as I'd always receive one randomly throughout the years. I mainly used it to read scriptures about worry and to help with sleeping. From a young age, I battled with not being able to shut my brain off and would often jolt up out of my sleep several times throughout the night in a panic state, worrying about the previous day's events/news. It could've been something exciting or something terrifying; either way, my brain tended to over-exaggerate everything. It was so annoying that I had to create different ways to find enough comfort to sleep.

I fell in love with daydreaming and classical music. I had a radio next to my bed, so at night, I'd turn my radio station from the pop station to the classical station. The sound of the instruments was soothing to my soul; it was like I could understand the language they spoke through the melodies. I would listen to the music every night, but some nights the music would be too dramatic, and it would interfere with my sleep. Once that happened, I would feel hopeless because what I identified as my safe haven soon became a nerve-wracking experience. See, I had to find a better way to drown out any noise that would be occurring outside of my bedroom. Whether that be my siblings making noise or my mom and her boyfriend fighting.

I made sure that my bedroom was something that made me, me, but most importantly, peaceful. Now back to the Bible, it was my number one source for going to sleep. I would turn to Genesis and start reading, but then I'd get sleepy quickly because the language was a little hard for me to understand. I had never taken any Bible study classes, and since I loved to learn and read, I thought that I'd take it upon myself to start. I was determined to read the whole Bible, but for some reason, I could never get through Genesis, so I always made sure that the Bible was under my pillow or on the other side of my bed as I slept. Two other things I did to fall asleep were put a knife under my pillow and daydream about my favorite boy band. Yes, I know what you're thinking, "How are you going to just speed past that knife situation?" Well, I felt unsafe in my home, but I knew that

God would keep me protected just in case he didn't get to me fast enough; I kept a knife for good measure. I knew that Jesus loved me. Why? Because the Bible tells me so. It was as simple as that for me to believe. I had to believe and dream big if I wanted to experience life beyond what I had been exposed to. So, from that young age, I made the decision to never stop dreaming.

Giving up on my dreams wasn't an option because, at 12, I was convinced that I needed to give up my life. This was the darkest time of my life, and as you can see, I've had dark times. But this darkness I was experiencing is so clear and to the point that I don't have much to share regarding the details because God spared my life and the details from resurfacing. At the age of 12, I recall being bombarded with roles and responsibilities that were beyond my comprehension during a time of grief. Grief from the loss of a loved one and my relationship with my father.

At the age of 11, I lost my favorite uncle, who died in a car crash. He was young, and the abandonment I felt from that was evident because he was an important part of my family's life. He was the fun uncle who made it a point to be active in all of our lives. I call him my favorite uncle because, as a child, I naturally had favorite people to whom I assigned those roles. My uncle was always present and more than my father, so losing him hurt deeply. But I didn't get a chance to grieve properly because shortly after his death, three of his children came to live with us. Let me put things into perspective for you; I was 11, had two siblings already, and my mother was pregnant with my third sibling. Taking more children into the home meant I had to watch, feed and clean up more than usual. Plus, losing their dad and being younger than me was a task on its own. They were used to seeing him every day, and then bam, they lost him, and their mother felt that she couldn't take care of them, so she gave my mother temporary custody. My cousin's lives were uprooted within a matter of days. My focus was on how challenging it had to have been for them, but the house was so busy that I didn't get much quiet time, and honestly, it was easy for me to step into nurturing mode. I can't honestly say that it was required of me to put my own feelings aside, but it was a behavior that I had learned to do because of previous life experiences. This transition lasted a month or two before their mother picked them up and moved them out of state with her. During this time, there was a lot, and I mean a lot of family drama. I was burnt out and just over life. I started to reflect on the unresolved grief from my grandmother passing away 7 years prior, and depression swept upon me and started taking over my thoughts and feelings to the point of no control.

While my living situation with my mom & her boyfriend was still dreadful, to make matters worse, my father decided to disappear. I recall, during this stage of my life, trying to get in contact with him but never receiving a response. A few months passed by, and my dad's sister informed my mother that he had relocated to the state that she lived in. When I heard this news, I was in complete shock. I had always known him to live in the same city as us, and although he didn't always keep his word when he told us he'd pick us up, he never went long without communicating with us.

Feelings of abandonment started to hit me deeper in this state because going over to my dad's house on the weekends or being with him and his family was an outlet for me. I was able to just be a kid and didn't have to worry about watching kids or being left alone. It felt like there was always something to do or people to be around whenever I was with my dad. But even when I look back at those times, he would drop us off at his family's home and wasn't always around when he had us. At the tender age of 12, I learned that someone could say they love you, but true love lies within their actions. I always learned that in this world, it's "every man for himself," meaning that I would always have to figure life out and that there was no way that I could rely on a mother or father to protect me. What I grew to learn as an adult is that God was there the entire time and that I could rely on him no matter what the circumstances were.

After battling with all these things, I decided to take measures into my own hands. There was no way that I was going to keep being talked down on, ignored, neglected and treated like I was unimportant by people. A thought popped up in my mind, which was the beginning of my relationship with suicidal thoughts. They were with me every time life became hard, any time that fear was heavy, and every time I felt like there was no resolution to my pain. They were present before I went to sleep and when I woke up. I dreaded being alive, so I decided I didn't have to be alive. I recall the evening of my suicide attempt; I had been feeling so much pain and burnout with life that nothing that usually made me feel better was helping. I loved music, reading, and writing, but none of it helped. I didn't feel safe talking to anyone, and God was the furthest from my mind at this time. So, I decided that it would be my last moment of living. Everyone was in the house sleeping, and it was evening, so I knew that I wouldn't be found until the morning. I picked up my bottle of Excedrin and took all the pills with a glass of water and lay down. I don't recall much, but I was knocked out fast. I don't recall thinking about anything; I just remember being at peace with the decision I was making.

Then, I felt a piercing pain in my head, and I started to move my body. I opened my eyes; it was morning time, with the sun shining brightly through my window. I was upset that I had lived to breathe another day. Then I realized that living must have been for a purpose. I started to ask God why he would let me live and not die because that's what I wanted at the time. It felt like it was so obvious as I heard a response telling me that my life was meaningful and that he would see me through it. It was like an instant agreement that I had with God. I told him that I wouldn't try anything like that again and that I trusted that he would help me. Now at that time, I was also under the impression that my grandmother was a guardian angel because who else could've wanted me alive?! That was the mind of my 12-year-old self. So, I woke up and prepared for school as usual and never shared my suicide attempt with anyone until adulthood. I feel like God delivered me from a demonic attack and gave me a fresh perspective on myself and life. From that day forward, I made a promise to live and not allow myself to die. I also made it a mission to seek peace in all that I did in life.

Now as a mother to a teen, I'm still dreaming big, bigger than I ever thought that I could. The little girl who was afraid to go to sleep learned that the fears couldn't hold her back and that she was bigger than the fear. That's how I broke free from every negative experience that tried to tell me otherwise. Fast forward to today, and I have successfully completed reading Genesis and most books in the bible at least 2 times or more! The power of reading for me is that I get to apply biblical lessons to my daily life and in the work that I do.

I was a master at being a victim and didn't realize just how destructive having that mindset was. My younger self experienced a great deal of pain, and allowing myself to be viewed as a victim kept me in a spiraling effect of allowing what others did to me to take root inside of me. It's as if each time a person violated, offended, shared information or misused me, there was a new seed planted in my mind of the event. Every time I remembered the event or experienced a new event like it, it was like me watering it to grow more. Before I knew it, I was getting to the root causes of why I had present day issues that required me to go back and see where they derived from. God helped me to do that. With him, I am nothing; because of him, I have my life!

### Prayer
Thank God for saving you from the attacks of the enemy, for his love for you and for giving you a long lifespan!

### Tip
Do not be ashamed to share your testimony of what the Lord has done for you. Be bold and loud; someone needs to hear it.

### Scripture
Psalms 91:14-15 (NIV) 14 "Because he loves me," says the LORD, "I will rescue him; I will protect him, for he acknowledges my name. 15 He will call on me, and I will answer him; I will be with him in trouble, I will deliver him and honor him.

## Chapter Nine

# Deliverance Is Free for All; He is Mighty!

I recall when I used to feel alone, sad, and shameful on Valentine's Day. There used to be moments when I didn't feel like I'd ever feel love. From what I recall, there haven't been many moments in my life that I've identified moments of true love until I started to build a relationship with God. I used to search high and low for love, and I was constantly "giving" love to everyone that came my way in hopes that they'd return it back to me. What I received was a pain in my heart and, in other cases, a knife in my back. The true meaning of love doesn't come from people; it comes from within. The moment I recognized that the weight to please others and rush to give them love faded. I was able to instantly recover from years of desperation. I can easily call it that now that I know the root cause of my ways. Me being real and authentic with myself has helped me to remove the mask that I once created to navigate through life. Did you know that it takes a lot to remove a mask that you didn't know you created? You must identify what made you create the mask and the layers that are connected to each phase of life. I feel like there are some things I'm still removing. The beauty in healing is that beauty never fades, the lack of self-awareness does, and we start to connect more with our true selves. God is still working on molding me; I feel like I'm in a state of quick elevation. Every week I'm learning something new about my purpose and building up the confidence to walk in my God-given authority. While I don't know what all of that will entail, I am excited about it.

When you give up your free will for God's will, be ready for him to work in unexpected supernatural ways that cannot be explained with human eyes. So today, I am choosing to live like I do any other day, be the best me that I can be, and work at the things I love to work at. Being single has taught me many things; if I'm operating out of desperation, trauma bonding with others, and desiring marriage, I will continue with the same cycle. I am choosing to be free from societal standards of being single and miserable. I am choosing to be single, whole, and preparing myself for marriage. I know that because it's my heart's desire, it shall come to pass; I must do what God has called me to do, and being obedient to doing life the way he designed will set me free from those past behaviors. While I'm still in the middle of my testimony, he has done just that in more ways than I could ever explain. I learned to understand that God's promises will not return to me void if I follow instructions. Once I learned that, I started to read my bible to learn about the instructions, first I focused on the sins, and then I learned about how he told us to present ourselves to others, and I came across this scripture: Ephesians 3:20 King James Version "Now unto him that is able to do exceeding abundantly above all that we ask or think, according to the power that worketh in us" I put my belief in the promise keeper and not the promise because that would easily lead me back into a state of desperation. I started to show up for myself every day by doing activities that made me feel good. I would take time off from work and say no to things that didn't make me feel well. I challenged myself to go above and beyond what I thought was impossible, and guess what? I did all the impossible things that my younger self could've ever imagined and more! That is what it looks like when you are diligently seeking the Lord and following his instructions; life becomes easier. Now although it's easier doesn't mean that there aren't some hard days.

    I have days when I don't want to write or see clients or parents; I just want to run away to an island with a beach. Whenever I have those days, I remind myself that I have peace in my home and peace in my heart, so I need to activate it instead of running to a place where the troubles will follow me too. It's impossible to take peace on vacation when stress doesn't stop because of the location. Life can be as sweet as you'd like it to be, so be bold, brave, and confident in the things that you do today so that your tomorrow has more hope. A scripture that comes to mind is: "Hope deferred makes the heart sick, but a longing fulfilled is a tree of life. Proverbs 13:12." Scripture has become part of my daily meditation; I make sure that whenever I am speaking to myself, I use biblical affirmations to jumpstart my day and carry the instructions throughout the day. I have come a long way; just in 2020, I only could recite Psalm 23, and in 2021 I started reading the bible every day. I jumped around from chapter to chapter before I started to put all the stories together. That's the interesting thing about being a baby Christian. You can start anywhere, but you grow in faith as you continue. Then as I watched a prophet on YouTube say, "Ask the Holy Spirit to guide you." It was at that moment my perspective of the stories I read in the bible changed. Then I started to change from the inside out. If you're reading this and you feel stuck, lonely, or unseen, keep going and do not stop; it will all make sense eventually! And at that moment, the mask will come off itself, and you will be glad that you kept your eyes on the promise keeper.

## Prayer
Ask the Holy Spirit to give you a revelation of the scripture you're reading before you begin.

## Tip
Find one scripture and recite it as many times a day as you can until you remember it. Repeat this step for other scriptures!

## Scripture
Proverbs 13:12 (KJV) Hope deferred maketh the heart sick: but when the desire cometh, it is a tree of life.

## Chapter Ten

# When You're Tired & Have Tried EVERYTHING, Try Jesus!

God has a way of delivering solutions to your problem that are individually designed. Many people grab resources from others who have healed, and after they've spent hundreds or thousands of dollars or hours watching other people's social media content, they still feel empty. This happens because people would rather lean on their own understanding than have faith in God. As sad as it sounds, it's happening more than usual. I mean, up until a few years ago, I was this person! Then I started building a relationship and had to start telling my problems that I serve a God who is the creator of the universe! Do you understand how major that is?! If you read Genesis 1, you will understand just how meaningful this is. He not only created the universe, humans, animals, etc., but he also made us in his own image. He also gave humans power and dominion over the earth. Wow, that is evidence that he loves us and can solve ANY problem we have. He's the manufacturer of our lives. But the reality is that it is easier to operate from a place of free will because we do not understand what that means for our life. It means we don't have the manual, aka instructions on navigating life.

Have you ever purchased an item from the store and tried to put the item together without reading the instructions? I have on many occasions, and the results were 50/50; either I put it together right on the first try, or I made a huge mistake and had to take it down and restart the process. While restarting the process, I would feel burnt out, irritable and displaced, but I would also sit down, pace myself and read the instructions so that I didn't make the same mistake the first time around. Imagine if we read the Holy Bible for advice to help us with making a decision. What if we read the bible to gain clarity on how God would handle a situation? What if we prayed and fasted before making any small or major decisions in life? It's easy to do these things out of a state of desperation, but what if we did it because we fear the Lord and desire to live how he wants us to live? That is the reality of operating in God's will and not our own. Not fearing the Lord is dangerous!

I recall a time in my life when I was desperate for God's voice and for him to hear me. I started watching people who I felt were honest and trustworthy people. I watched their videos daily and purchased their services and products. I allowed myself to be consecrated in God's word and the words he had given them to help set people like me free. I did this for years and years before I realized that their blueprint wouldn't save me. The whole issue with this is that I was studying their blueprint instead of studying the one who gave them the blueprint. I wasted money, time, and effort trying to become what I thought God wanted me to be. I was receiving ideas from God on who he wanted me to be, but that didn't mean that he was telling me to be like others. The power of God is that he can put something right in front of our faces that our human brains will only take in what we see rather than what God is saying while he's presenting it to us. Building a relationship with God allows the Holy Spirit to convict us when we are making poor choices or give us confirmation when we are on the right path. This is why it's so important to implement the Holy Bible into your daily life. It allows you to know what's right and what's wrong. When you look at social media or spend time with the people in your community, you will automatically think that how the world operates is acceptable to God. Why? Because trends are considered normal and appropriate for many cultures. When you decide to operate in God's will, you must be willing to let go of cultures and only follow Christ. Cultures waver, and trends within cultures fade. God's will and promises will never fade; they always remain the same (Isaiah 55:11).

I recall a time when I thought that I had misheard what God told me. Well, to be truthful, this has happened on multiple occasions. During my walk with the Lord, I have been rebellious and had unbelief, which I've had to repent for each time. When I reflect on why I was rebellious, it is because I wanted to see things from the perspective of what I had experienced in life. As I was reading the Bible, I noticed a pattern in God's love for his people because anytime a group or nation of people was under attack, he sent a servant of his to warn the people. That warning would also come with instructions. God always gave me a warning with instruction, but because I wasn't accustomed to this kind of love, I took it lightly. The dangers of taking it lightly meant that I was walking onto a path of destruction without preparation. The tools that the Lord tried to give to me were handed over to me, but I decided to drop them. That immediately sent me into a spiritual war without armor. Did you know that God made us a promise to never leave us nor forsake us? He states that very clearly.

See, God's directions are clear and straight to the point. That is a form of love. I was so accustomed to confusion that I started to rationalize God's instructions and create my own. What I now know is that God knows and sees what I can't see; I was blinded because when he was trying to give me the instructions, I was silencing his voice. I was cutting off the communication line, which made me a weak vessel in the battle. I was attacked on so many occasions that I am still recovering from those attacks today. This is how disobedience can impact us, and the consequences aren't always severe, but they are necessary. Necessary for growth so that the lesson doesn't have to repeat itself.

I have often seen testimonies of individuals recovering from a terminal Illness. The Bible highlights many people being healed from infirmities and deformities. While I didn't have any severe illnesses, I used to identify myself as being my mother's "sickly child." It seemed as if I was the only one battling with some type of pain, virus, and random disorder. When I got sick, it felt like a life-or-death situation. I recall my sick episodes starting off with a simple dry cough to feeling like my chest was burning on fire. If I was around a person for a short time, I would easily catch their cold. My body would be so sore and in pain that I would have to push through it just to get it out of the way. Meaning I would take medications and rest, hoping that after the third day of being sick, I would soon start to feel better. This became part of the norm for me throughout the years before I realized how unnatural it was to get sick that often. I was told by doctors that I had a weakened immune system. Even though I didn't understand it fully, I took ownership of it, and that's exactly why I started to have a lower immune system more and more over time. I started having migraines at a young age as well. I would keep a bottle of Excedrin on my nightstand because they were that routine. Having migraines and a common cold throughout my adolescence brought me much discomfort as I was not able to sleep or spend as much time doing the things that I enjoyed. Even if I didn't feel well, I grew a relationship with my pain where I tolerated it and normalized it to the point of feeling numb. That's how powerful the brain is. I used to push through the pain, but do you know how abnormal it is for a teen to normalize pushing through pain? I learned to push through the pain of my physical health. I learned to push through the pain of my emotional pain. I learned to push through mental pain. I was just pushing through and pushing through but never understanding the underlying issues. Do you know that the longer you push through, the deeper the pain gets over time, and the more the infection of the pain grows with you? When you hear the saying "Time heals all wounds," I am here to tell you that is not true; it's a false statement. I couldn't communicate my pain at that age because I had already obtained a perspective that my issues didn't matter and that I needed to figure it out on my own. The problem with having that mentality is that it damages my ability to understand my own needs. I then picked up the habit of focusing on others' needs and helping them to problem solve. I found great pleasure in this because it was one of the strategies for me to numb my issues to push through the pain. See how damaging it was for me to navigate that way as a kid? I carried this perspective with me throughout my 20s until I hit 30. By this time, I started formulating the importance of growing older but looking and feeling younger. When I hit the age of 29, I started to feel the random aches and pains that I heard came with the age of 30. I didn't like it one bit, so I decided to pick up books, watch YouTube videos and follow the testimonies of others who healed themselves from severe illnesses. Mind you, I didn't have a severe illness. I was just tired of hearing the doctors tell me that my immune system was low without giving me a strategy to build my immune system up besides using vitamins.

I am saying this with great confidence, try Jesus. Give him a chance to show you what he was designed to do. He didn't make the sacrifices for us to lose; he made the sacrifices for us to win. Victory is a God-given authority. I wasn't operating in that authority due to a lack of faith, awareness, and foolishness. But God has an awesome way of turning things around right when you feel like you're drowning or falling off the edge. Drowning in debt? Call Jesus for a strategy to be a better steward of your finances. Having relationship issues? Evaluate your relationship with Jesus so that he can shape and mold you to be a better person. Feel like you're losing your mind? Call on Jesus, as he is the ultimate healer.

### Prayer
Thank God for his clear instructions and for giving you grace and mercy when you didn't follow through with the instructions.

### Tip
Learn the difference between God's voice, your own voice, and the enemy's. Learning the difference between the three will help you strengthen and elevate how you hear and follow God.

### Scripture
Proverbs 16:20 (NIV) Whoever gives heed to instruction prospers, and blessed is the one who trusts in the LORD.

## Chapter Eleven

# The Power of Repentance

I often hear how repenting should be a lifestyle. I didn't realize it until I made God a promise and failed to keep it due to my lack of self-control. But what happens when you lack awareness of the truth of your reality? The reality is that you have more control over your life's destiny than you think. It's far beyond what you or many others could have imagined and thought. When I gained a closer relationship with God, I learned that, as a human, I was making life more complicated than it needed to be. I understood that I was making poor choices and felt great suffering due to a lack of knowledge.

"Hosea 4:6 (KJV) My people are destroyed for lack of knowledge: because thou hast rejected knowledge, I will also reject thee, that thou shalt be no priest to me: seeing thou hast forgotten the law of thy God, I will also forget thy children."

We live in a society where the people we see in the world glorify everything that God tells us not to do. It's hard to escape, but this is why we must have standards and values that we follow in life; if not, it leads up to having a "follow the leader" mentality. It decreases us from having a voice or control over making decisions. Many people are being given the option to make a decision, but because they are given 1-2 options, they grow to learn that the options are typically two evils. I've heard the saying "choose the lesser of the two evils" many times in life and felt that if those were the options, then I would choose none.

I grew up in a family that identified as Christian but didn't display Christian behaviors. My option to choose how I lived came from me comparing what I saw on tv versus my reality. Honestly, neither were great options because television shows were for entertainment purposes only. Learning from tv shows caused me to make more assumptions about life. I viewed it from a child's state of mind and from a trauma perspective. I watched many family shows that showed a father in the home, but I don't recall my father ever living in the home before the age of 17 or having a healthy relationship with my mother. I later learned they did reside together until I was about 4 years old. I saw them constantly arguing and manipulating each other while co-parenting.

It wasn't until I was 17 that they started a relationship again, and he lived in the home for a short time. During that time, I realized I had dreamed about us all living under one roof and having my parents married. I was drastically shocked when they showed me the reason why it was good for them to be separated all those years. I hadn't thought about this experience until now. It was one of the biggest misconceptions about life that impacted my ability to dream big about relationships. While my father was living with us, it felt like he was more of a roommate. The division was heavy and chaotic. He was minimal when interacting with me and my siblings.

When I look back at that experience, it showed me how not to do relationships. The tv shows left me feeling confused as I didn't have the role of the proper step modeled in front of me to understand the results I longed for. So overall, I put pressure on myself to figure it out on my own; the problem is I had to suffer to learn that I needed God's help, grace, love, forgiveness, and more to understand the true meaning of a healthy family life. Overall, this was the suffering that I endured because of my family turning their back on God. I understand that and accept it. I also decided that I wanted to break the chains that were over my life because of my family's rejection of the Lord through repentance. I decided that I would repent for sins I didn't commit but for sins that were committed by every ancestor that came before me. When I say EVERY, I mean every. Even if the sun was far beyond anything I would've ever done, I repented. I know it sounds crazy to take ownership of something that you didn't do. I challenge you to think about the ownership the enemy has over you because of the guilty charges. If the bloodline is cursed, what are you willing to do to break the curse? Pride can stand in the way of that because it feeds the curse. Hosea speaks about repenting, and this requires humility. Why? Because God gave specific instructions for us to follow. He gives us the option of free will or God's will. I learned that all of my life, I had been operating from my own will. Once I took inventory of the fruit from doing my own will, I realized I had a fruitless life. I'd take it a step further to say that my life was like the cursed fig tree from the Bible. Now picture a fig tree. It's being watered and has sunlight but produces nothing. It has no meaning. I was operating from my own free will and not producing anything but more fruitless memories, relationships, and future goals.

Throughout my life, I ran to the Bible when I needed encouragement or to alleviate anxiety. I didn't read the Bible when I was happy and content. I wasn't aware that reading the Bible would unlock answers that people couldn't give me. After years of depending on others for knowledge, I started to be intentional about reading the Bible at the age 34. At the age of 33, I kept hearing and reading stories on social media of Jesus dying at the same age. I was terrified because that was a fear I had since I was a young girl, dying young. I guess this was the awakening of my returning home to him. If I was to put things into a different perspective now, I can see that that era of my life was dying and that I'd be led into a new era; this time, I would be walking with Jesus instead of against him.

As I began learning and building a relationship with God, it dawned on me that there were many ways of living that I had normalized. The moment that God showed me the errors in my ways was the moment that I started to struggle with the concept of free will versus God's will. I would like to say that I jumped all in and gave my life over to Christ, but I did a tug of war with myself before I understood the bigger picture of his will. I would read and understand the importance of sex in marriage but had already been operating outside of that for so long that lust had a strong hold over me. It made me mentally go back and forth between doing God's will or my own. I know God had made it very clear to me that I needed to abstain, but it didn't make sense to my flesh. The flesh will fool you every time if you allow it. I learned the hard way that the world operated out of their free will and flesh, which naturally rejected God's will. The one thing that helped me was correction. Hearing others on social media advocating for abstinence until marriage and sharing their testimonies about it helped me to see that it was possible. I needed faith to carry me, not another strategy to abstain; that's the easy part. It was hard for me to believe and visualize what it would look like because I had never seen it. If I did see it, it was being displayed from a fear-based perspective, and that's just as damaging as the other. Although correction works for me, many become offended when their poor behavior is corrected, which creates more issues in life. The spirit of offense opens the door to pride, anger, unforgiveness, and much more. I had to decide which way of living I desired to live. Once I chose Christ, I chose life, and he guided me on the understanding that choosing him looks different from how I used to live life and how the world lives. For me, the correction was understanding the error in my ways, learning why they were errors, and how to no longer operate from that place of error. God guided me through all of this as I prayed, fasted, read the Bible, and allowed the Holy Spirit to guide me. "Psalms 34:17 (KJV) The righteous cry, and the LORD heareth, and delivereth them out of all their troubles."

When I took the initiative to follow God, that naturally meant that I had to leave the world; leaving the world for me meant that I had to let go of an identity that I had grown very familiar with. I had to go through several phases of being stripped. I feel like today, there is still some stripping taking place. The difference between a few years ago and now is that I am a willing participant in the stripping. Stripping builds characteristics such as faith, forgiveness, and integrity, among many other things. It strips away hate, envy, lust, disloyalty, fear, and procrastination. The stripping is intense and painful. There are days when I must rest and let go of my usual activities to fully operate without resistance to the stripping. Gone are the days that I overwork myself trying to avoid the side effects of stripping. After the cycle is done, I tend to feel like a new person with fresh ideas, energy, and courage. I feel bold in my faith and actively operate within it.

See, I've learned a few things about God. He makes no mistakes, and he can be gentle with his approach to shaping and molding us. But it requires a willing participant to make the process the easiest. Now, I didn't say it was easy, but as a human, I know how complicated we can make things when we operate from a place of resistance.

While following God is tough, owning up to our own sins can be much more complicated, so here are some things that we should repent for:

- Allowing ourselves to be programmed by the tv, news, movie, and social media that opposes God's word.
- Allowing other systems to raise our children and putting more time and energy into building up a business for income.
- Procrastination and laziness as it will require time and effort to build a relationship with God to gain an understanding of who he is and his plan and purpose for you.
- Craving instant gratification and engaging in impulsive behaviors.
- Dismissing God when he gave an instruction.
- Having unbelief in your heart.
- And every sin you can think of that you and your ancestors have participated in!

While this is a short list, it will help us all to become better stewards of the life that God has given us and avoid participating in things that keep us from God.

### Prayer
Thank God for forgiving you.

### Tip
Be sure to forgive any and everyone who has caused you any hurt!

### Scripture
Matthew 6:14 (KJV) For if ye forgive men their trespasses, your heavenly Father will also forgive you:

## Chapter Twelve

# Don't Delay Your Deliverance

The power of deliverance is a supernatural experience that can only be understood through having a relationship with God. For most of my life, my relationship looked like me having random conversations with him, listening to some of his instructions for my life and sitting in his presence sporadically. I didn't understand that having an in-and-out relationship with him was causing me to miss out on who he was. The reason that I had not had a divine, routine encounter with God the way that I could have been because of my life choices. I chose to only focus on the things that I could see. I was wrapped up in working a job, attending school and raising a son. I thought that those were the only tasks that were important as I was navigating adulthood. I had not seen a person prioritize God in their lives outside of seeing people in the church, but I didn't see their life behind the scenes. When I look back at the people I encountered with a relationship with God, I often wonder why they didn't pull me aside and minister to me. I had some people hint at having a child out of wedlock but never discuss how it would impact my life over time, most importantly, how God views fornication. I can admit that I was headstrong in my young adult years and felt that I knew a lot, but I only was headstrong because I had to be, not because I wanted to be.

When I think of the church and Christians growing up, I do not remember receiving attention from them. I recall feeling alone and not seen. Actually, this is how I've felt the majority of my life with everyone in my life. I was so busy making sure that I was seeing and hearing everyone else that I didn't know that I was projecting onto them what I needed for myself. Wow, what a revelation to have. This is why it's so important to have a relationship with God. He reveals things to you to help with healing by directly delivering to you or giving you a strategy to be delivered from a thing. Imagine trying to heal chest pain but not knowing the root cause of the pain. Naturally, with physical health concerns, we schedule an appointment with a doctor. Once at the appointment, we inform them of our medical history and recent symptoms. We then go through a series of exams and labs that help the doctor determine what is taking place on the inside of our bodies. Then we are given a treatment recommended by the doctor. Most people follow the plan, and then there are others who do not, and they must suffer through the symptoms. The suffering can last for days, and it can lead up to years, depending on the severity of the condition. I would often ask myself, "Why would a person suffer when they could just listen to the doctor's orders and be healed?"

This is something that I am still trying to wrap my head around today. But God makes no mistakes; we as people do, and we can make poor choices due to allowing our flesh to think for us rather than using logic to make the best choices.

The way that people go to the doctor and choose to suffer in the same way that people who do not go to God for healing suffer from spiritual pain. I view spiritual pain as having issues with the following: a lack of purpose, low sense of self, poor self-esteem, confusion, double-mindedness, fear, anxiety, depression, suicide, abandonment, rejection and all unseen symptoms that only can be described through a person's behaviors and verbal report. I'd also take it a step further to say that the outcomes, aka the fruit of their lives, are also a great indicator that a person is going through spiritual pains.

I know of a Great Physician that can heal all things, not some, but all. While it's not always an easy process, it requires patience and diligence to break down the pain and restore it. I feel that some can be healed overnight while others take time. Just like the body can heal itself, our spirits can be healed naturally as well. It's all about supplying our minds, body, spirits and souls with the proper nutrition and environment for them to restore themselves and thrive. Often, we try to operate in the same way that we did before we became aware of the spiritual pains. The problem is that we are encouraging the pain to thrive under the same circumstances that birthed it. As a therapist, if I were to tell a client to maintain life as it was before their suicidal or depressive episode, that would negate the need for therapy. People come because they want to understand why and how they arrived at the point of having uncontrolled emotional distress. It would be necessary for me to support them by highlighting the significant thoughts, behaviors and perspectives that need to be addressed. It's also important that they understand what's within their control. Oftentimes we as people will focus on the pieces of our lives that we would like to change instead of putting effort towards the things that are within our control. God gives us freedom over certain decisions that we make in life; that's called free will. Then we have access to living under his will for our lives, which can sometimes be counterproductive to our own will. Nevertheless, his will is always best. But there comes a time in our lives when we must let go of our own free will to free ourselves from our own suffering. The type of suffering that God never meant for us to endure. When we allow God to heal us, he gives us strategies on what to do. When I was being healed from an opus thinking, one of my strategies for me was to listen to soft, classical music while reciting the scripture "casting all your care upon him; for he careth for you."

While I didn't understand why he'd have me do this when I was taught to reframe negative thoughts, I decided to trust him. For me, that was major because I had never thought to trust anyone or situation with my emotional and mental wellbeing. But he was teaching me something that was going to be a prescription for the issues I was having. I had tried the medications, working out, deep breathing and going outside in nature but never had I applied the word of God to my life to cast out anything that shouldn't be present. God told me to do it nightly before bed because that was the time that was the hardest for me. My mind would start wandering about all of life's expectations and experiences. It always felt like a never-ending cycle of memories that I just could not shake. I realized just how real the statement is "An idle mind is the devil's playground." I felt like I was opening myself up to flashbacks and fears that weren't productive for where I was presently, and God was showing me where I needed to be. So, my nighttime routines became peaceful because I would have conversations with God, sharing all my dreams, and he would comfort me with reminders about the scriptures he had been leading me to recite. I then understood the power of devouring my spirit with the word of God. It was a supernatural experience when God lifted the heaviness of anxiety I had been carrying for years. I had only known life with it, and now that I was able to live life without it, I felt a renewal in my mind and in all areas of life!

That's the power of God that many have yet to encounter, and some may never experience it before leaving this earth. It took me over 30 years for me to learn that, and my prayer is that I can help others so that it doesn't take them over 30 years to figure it out. So far, I am on the right track; as of today, I've worked with over 350 people in my private practice alone, and I haven't counted how many people I've inspired through my posts, videos and courses online. When you are delivered, you will immediately want to share and tell EVERYONE. It's 2023, and I have been sharing left and right nonstop with those who have ears to listen. Now, there have been many encounters with people who reject my testimony, but I know for certain that they can't deny my testimony. The beauty of being delivered is that while you are sharing your journey, you are planting a seed of hope. Hope that the person who hears it will become curious enough to discover Jesus on their own without pressuring them. I can recall moments when it was obvious that I was talking too much about my testimony that others became uncomfortable or overwhelmed with me sharing. I have learned that me sharing my journey isn't for their comfort but to glorify God. If he is pleased with me, then that is all that matters. I often hear that people don't talk enough about God and how he's delivered them. I am encouraging everyone to cry aloud and spare not about the impact of sins, the importance of repenting, and the effects of deliverance. It's a beautiful and rough journey, but we must be on one according to birth, the results on earth that God has called us to help him with.

While deliverance is free for all, many do not desire to go through deliverance. They would prefer to satisfy their flesh than to have eternal life. I have seen it on countless occasions where people will know God's word but reject it by not following it behind closed doors. It appears to me that people love to use God's word for their own gain but not apply it for the gain of God in their lives. If they only knew how much more they could do in life when God is at the head of their lives, they would make wise choices. But we live in a society where people love instant gratification from the world, and with God, gratification is a choice to feel satisfied whether we have materialistic things or not. So, if you had to choose whether to go through deliverance, I encourage you to take the path of self-deliverance. That's what I did! A matter of praying, fasting, and scripture will help you connect with a ministry that can guide you through this journey and be prepared for the stripping!

**Prayer**
Thank God for his grace and mercy.

**Tip**
Give your all to God, not some all!

**Scripture**
Galatians 5:1 (KJV) Stand fast therefore in the liberty wherewith Christ hath made us free, and be not entangled again with the yoke of bondage.

## Chapter Thirteen

# Friendships Change After Deliverance

Friendships were snatched away from me left and right when I started to grow spiritually, and honestly, I'm glad! I decided that the journey of walking with Christ was most important. There were things that I accepted from friends that God started to show me were unacceptable as his child. The more I started to accept the changes I had to make within myself, the more I became irritable with the behaviors that I saw in others. It was a feeling of disgust; it was more of a lack of understanding of how a person could be that way. But God started to show me that these were the hidden behaviors that I had that I wasn't aware of myself. That led me to understand the scientific theory of "like attracts like." I could no longer look at others and see their problems, but I had to evaluate what was going on internally for me to uproot the problems. I used to have a friend that was harsh when it came to how they responded to others' poor decision-making skills. They were blunt and so upfront to the point that they were the definition of a mean girl. To me, it was cool when they were doing it to others, but when it was my turn, it hurt. Especially since I was that friend who would show up to support them at any given time. As I started to heal, I would hear her constantly talking down about her exes and other people who had hurt her. It was excessive to the point that she would keep repeating the same conversations with me each time we talked. After getting off the phone with her, I would feel intense fatigue, which would last days. Then it hit me that there's no way that she doesn't do this same thing with other friends regarding me. The gossipy behavior was too much for me to ignore how often she did it, and it was with every friend she had. I decided to cut back on what I shared by only sharing positive news. I expected her to be super encouraging the way that I was towards her, but it resulted in her putting doubtful thoughts in my mind. I know that my dreams can be pretty big, but I felt that because I envisioned that it would come to fruition one day. I mean, I was working full-time in my business at this point, so if a girl like me could make it that far, then I could go even further! But that's the point that God wanted me to see that no matter what ideas he has given me, do not allow the opinions of others to interfere with believing his word. I had to learn the true meaning of trusting God despite what those that I loved had to say. And trust me, she wasn't the only one who had something to say.

I then learned the power of having friendships that complement me rather than holding onto history and bonds that were created from trauma. While we had a lot in common based on our upbringing and even our early adulthood, something shifted where my life path changed from being right in alignment with hers to being completely different. It felt like it happened overnight, but it was during a traumatic breakup that started to open my eyes to a lot of things. Our best bonding moments were when I was going through a breakup. Now that told me a lot, the relationship couldn't stand the test of time because eventually, I'd be healed, and if she wasn't willing to work on her healing, then I'd be bound to her forever. I decided that the cycle wasn't productive, so God gave me the go to let it go emotionally, and that naturally shifted physically. I didn't call her, and she would call me every 6-8 months until I just didn't return a missed phone call to her one time. As petty as this may sound, I did have a conversation with her at least a year prior to the full disconnection where I was honest about how I felt about being on a different path and feeling that it was necessary to dissolve the relationship. Ok, I didn't put it into those words, but she got the hint and only called 1-2 times a year, which was great for me until I had a full revelation of who

God called me to be. And he showed me that through a dream that included her.

In the dream, I was watching a play about what it looks like to be in a school. Then I looked in the row in front of me; I saw her communicating with a person who she was close to sharing my intimate secrets. In the dream, it was obvious that it was something that she was doing that was wrong, so when I woke up, I dove deeper into asking the Holy Spirit what it represented. The Holy Spirit confirmed that she was sharing personal information with someone who wasn't trustworthy but also that the friend that I had wasn't trustworthy. I recall telling this friend that I was no longer interested in knowing about the other person and that I was choosing to no longer associate myself with them because of their false identity. The friend then proceeded to normalize that was how the person was and to ignore their poor behavior. The problem with this is that I had already decided to show up as my best self and to only associate myself with people of integrity. I was learning that the friend I grew apart from was more like the people I chose not to be around. It was the gift of discernment that I was growing to have, thanks to God and the distance from the friend that helped to pull the wool from over my eyes. I was thankful that God showed me the truth about this person so I could stop running to them to share information. So, growing my relationship with God allowed me to make better decisions. I told myself that if God wasn't at the head of the relationship, then I didn't want it. I had seen first-hand what it was like to walk out of his presence. I am determined to remain in his presence!

Letting go of friends God has instructed you to release will give you time to step back and evaluate the relationship. God was able to inform me of all the things that made the friendships wrong for me and how they weren't in alignment with his plans for me. See how that works? I may have had plans for my life, including the people in it, that I didn't understand that before I had a plan, God had one! His plans are always better. I've never seen a plan that I set for myself become better than what God had in store for me. Releasing outdated relationships allows you to be led by God on a fresh perspective into the meaning of a true friendship.

### Prayer
Ask God which relationships need to be released to maintain your deliverance. And which friendships should remain and how to strengthen them.

### Tip
Identify healthy ways to grow with this change.

### Scripture
Proverbs 27:17 (KJV) Iron sharpeneth iron; so a man sharpeneth the countenance of his friend.

## Chapter Fourteen

# What Are You Willing to Sacrifice for Your FREEDOM?

The decisions that we make in life naturally pull us towards sacrificing our lives for the world or a sacrifice to fulfill a purpose. One decision will lead to eternal death, while the other leads to death in the flesh but eternal life. On many occasions, I had to stop myself from thinking that a temporary pleasure meant more than the reward of pleasing God. Eventually, it became a no-brainer for me to always choose God because, with him, I will always win. Even on my low days and when it looks like I'm losing, I'm truly winning. You must know that God will not abandon or reject a child he has chosen and a child who has chosen to diligently seek his face. He doesn't abandon the broken-hearted or the ones who lift up his name.

There are no boundaries to God's love when you're in covenant with him. He will go through whatever measure to keep you safe and thriving when you follow his instructions. Following him leads to eternal freedom, no longer being held captive by your circumstances.

Listen, the best thing that I ever could've done was lay down my life for God to give me a new one. Dying to oneself is no easy task, but one thing that I know and two things for certain, I was living a life that wasn't bearing me any good fruit. You must get to a point in life where you are tired of being dragged by the enemies' assignment over your life. You must be willing to let go of the old so that you can obtain the new. You cannot be two things at once. Let me make this clearer; you cannot operate from your old mindset and integrate a new mindset into the mix. I call that being double-minded because you won't know the true nature of what it's like to be renewed because you are still carrying around old baggage.

God is not an author of confusion. He makes things very clear to us, but it's up to us to decide if we want to live or die. I was tired of dying mentally, emotionally, spiritually, financially, and relationally. Have you ever had something molded in your fridge or trash, and it left a stench odor in the home? That's the kind of discomfort I felt from all the areas of my life that were dead. I had to get to the point where I wanted to live, and that came from me dying in the flesh. Yes, that's right. I had to deny my flesh of worldly things that were not acceptable to God. If you are aware of the commandments in the Bible, then you are aware that it can be easy to operate in sins that are normalized by humans. If you haven't read the Bible or have challenges with understanding it, attend a Bible study class to gain more understanding of it, but most importantly, partner with the Holy Spirit to guide you!

www.ingramcontent.com/pod-product-compliance
Lightning Source LLC
Chambersburg PA
CBHW061730070526
44583CB00024B/3075